10/04

Jacqueline Farmer

# Pumpkins

## Illustrated by Phyllis Limbacher Tildes

Charlesbridge

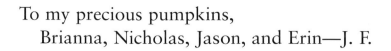

To my precious pumpkins,
    Brianna, Nicholas, Jason, and Erin—J. F.

For my nephews,
    Philip and Derek Limbacher, with love—P. L. T.

Published by Charlesbridge
85 Main Street
Watertown, MA 02472
(617) 926-0329
www.charlesbridge.com

**Library of Congress Cataloging-in-Publication Data**
Farmer, Jacqueline.
    Pumpkins / Jacqueline Farmer ; illustrated by Phyllis Limbacher Tildes.
        p. cm.
Summary: Presents a history of pumpkins, how they are grown, their
nutritional value, and recipes using pumpkin.
    ISBN 1-57091-557-1 (reinforced for library use)
    ISBN 1-57091-558-X (softcover)
    1.  Pumpkin—Juvenile literature. [1. Pumpkin.]  I. Tildes, Phyllis
Limbacher, ill. II. Title.
    SB347.F37 2004
    635'.62—dc22                                   2003015847

Printed in Korea
(hc)  10 9 8 7 6 5 4 3 2 1
(sc)  10 9 8 7 6 5 4 3 2 1

Illustrations done in watercolor and pencil on illustration board
Type set in Lemonade, Garamouche, and Sabon
Color separated, printed, and bound by Sung In Printing, Korea
Production supervision by Brian G. Walker
Designed by Susan Mallory Sherman

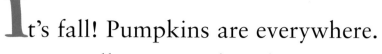

It's fall! Pumpkins are everywhere.

From Halloween jack-o'-lanterns to Thanksgiving pie, the pumpkin is star of the show. When the jack-o'-lantern smiles, we smile, too!

The pumpkin is a fruit, not a vegetable. Like all fruits, it has seeds inside that can grow into new pumpkin plants. Pumpkins, like cucumbers, melons, and squash, belong to the Cucurbita (kew-KUR-bi-tuh) group. Because the pumpkin grows from a single pistil, a small part of the flower, it's not just a fruit. It is also a berry.

Here are just a few kinds of pumpkins.

Pumpkins come in red, white, and even blue!

The Connecticut Field is grown for carving, not eating.

The sweet Small Sugar makes a blue-ribbon pie.

A Jack-Be-Little can fit in your hands.

An Atlantic Giant pumpkin may weigh more than your whole family!

People in Latin America have been eating pumpkins for a long time. In Mexico, pumpkin seeds more than 11,000 years old have been found in caves. In Peru and Mexico there are beautiful pots shaped like pumpkins!

For hundreds of years, Native Americans grew pumpkins for food and medicine. The pumpkin family, beans, and corn were called The Three Sisters. The Iroquois Indians believed these important crops were gifts from God.

In 1620 the *Mayflower* Pilgrims arrived in what is now Massachusetts. During the first winter, nearly half of them starved to death. In the spring of 1621, the Patuxet chief Squanto taught the survivors to plant pumpkins. The fruit was special because it stayed fresh through the long winter when stored in a root cellar.

The Pilgrims sprinkled pumpkin seeds among the corn and fertilized them with fish. Squanto showed them that growing corn and pumpkins together was good for both crops. The pumpkin plant's large leaves kept weeds away and helped keep the soil moist.

For many years Americans ate lots of pumpkin! Then, at the end of the 19th century, refrigeration was invented. People didn't need root cellars anymore because the refrigerator kept food fresh. So people didn't eat as much pumpkin.

Today, nine out of ten of the pumpkins people buy are used to make jack-o'-lanterns.

Every year more than one hundred million pumpkins are grown on large farms in the United States.

Growing pumpkins takes lots of water and fertilizer. Farmers loosen the soil so that air and rainwater can reach the roots of the pumpkin plants. Then they add animal manure or other fertilizers. Finally, when the soil is warm, they plant the pumpkin seeds.

Pumpkins are 90 percent water. Because weeds take water away from the plant, farmers pull out every weed they see. Sometimes black plastic is stretched over the soil under the young plants. This prevents weeds and keeps the soil moist, too.

Soon, beautiful flowers appear. Each pumpkin plant has both male and female blossoms. Bees carry pollen from the male flower to the female flower. This is called pollination. After pollination the bump at the base of the female flower begins to grow into a pumpkin. It will grow for 80 to 120 days. By mid-October the fruit is ready for picking—just in time for Halloween!

While most pumpkins are grown on farms, some gardeners grow them in their own backyards. Many people plant the new, smaller varieties of pumpkins. Others like to grow old-fashioned pumpkins, called "heirloom" varieties—the same kinds their grandparents grew.

But a few gardeners just want to grow a prize-winning GIANT pumpkin! They pamper their pumpkins with huge amounts of water, fertilizer, and time. Some even give them names like Goliath, King Kong, or Tarzan. Others think that playing music for their plants will help them grow bigger.

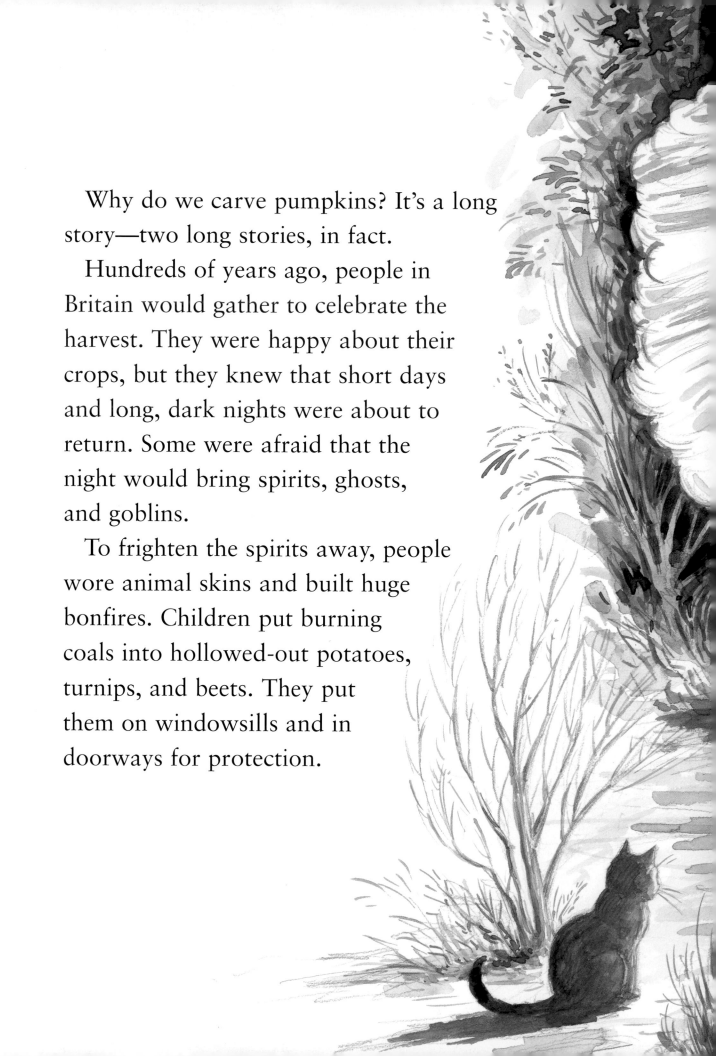

Why do we carve pumpkins? It's a long story—two long stories, in fact.

Hundreds of years ago, people in Britain would gather to celebrate the harvest. They were happy about their crops, but they knew that short days and long, dark nights were about to return. Some were afraid that the night would bring spirits, ghosts, and goblins.

To frighten the spirits away, people wore animal skins and built huge bonfires. Children put burning coals into hollowed-out potatoes, turnips, and beets. They put them on windowsills and in doorways for protection.

The name "jack-o'-lantern" comes from an Irish folktale about a foolish man named Stingy Jack. Jack played tricks on the devil, which made the devil really angry.

When Jack died, the devil didn't want him. But heaven didn't want him either, so Jack was forced to wander the earth forever. To light his way, he carved a lantern out of a turnip and placed a burning coal inside. People called him "Jack of the Lantern" or just "Jack-o'-Lantern."

In America today, people carve jack-o'-lanterns just for fun. But now they use pumpkins instead of turnips. Not only are pumpkins easier to carve, but big pumpkin jack-o'-lanterns are much scarier.

Try to carve your own jack-o'-lantern. Choose a pumpkin with an interesting shape and a flat bottom. To make a lid, draw a circle around the stem. Then draw a face on your pumpkin with a felt-tip pen.

With an adult's help, cut along the line around the stem. Point the knife toward the center. This will keep the lid from falling into the pumpkin. Be sure the opening is big enough for your hand to fit through.

Scoop out the seeds and all the stringy, slimy, yucky stuff. Save the seeds for toasting!

Then, with an adult's help, cut along the lines, making sure each cut goes all the way through the shell. Triangles are easy to cut for the eyes and nose. Be careful! If the holes are too close together, the spaces between may collapse. You can fix any breaks with toothpicks.

Have an adult help you place the candle inside the pumpkin so it won't fall over. After lighting the candle for the first time, punch a small hole inside the lid where the flame has burned the flesh black. This chimney will help to keep the candle burning. Sprinkle cinnamon or nutmeg inside the lid. When the candle is lit, the jack-o'-lantern will smell like pumpkin pie.

To keep your jack-o'-lantern looking fresh, rub the cut edges with petroleum jelly and store it in a cool place. A refrigerator works well, if your pumpkin is small enough to fit.

Pumpkins aren't just for carving. They are also a health food. Pumpkins have lots of vitamin A, which is good for your eyes, skin, teeth, and bones, and vitamin C, which helps the body fight infection.

Pumpkins can be made into butter, cookies, breads, and puddings. They can be roasted or whipped into ice cream. But it's pumpkin pie that we love best.

An early recipe for pumpkin pie might have looked like this:

Remove top of a small, sweet pumpkin.
Scoop out all seeds.
Fill shell with milk and molasses.
Add peeled, chopped apples (optional).
Stir in spices.
Bake near hot coals, till done.

This modern pumpkin pie is really yummy. Try it with an adult's help.

## Pumpkin–Maple Pie

One 16-ounce can of pure pumpkin
1 cup whipping cream
¾ cup pure maple syrup
3 large eggs
1 tablespoon all-purpose flour
½ teaspoon maple flavoring
1 teaspoon pumpkin pie spice
Pinch of salt
One unbaked 9-inch piecrust

Preheat oven to 350 degrees. Whisk all of the ingredients in a bowl.
Pour the filling into the unbaked crust. Bake 55 minutes, or until
the filling is set.

Pumpkin seeds have lots of fiber, vitamin E, vitamin B, iron, and protein.

Toasting the seeds with spices makes a simple, tasty, and healthy treat. Toasting also makes the hull, or shell, easier to remove.

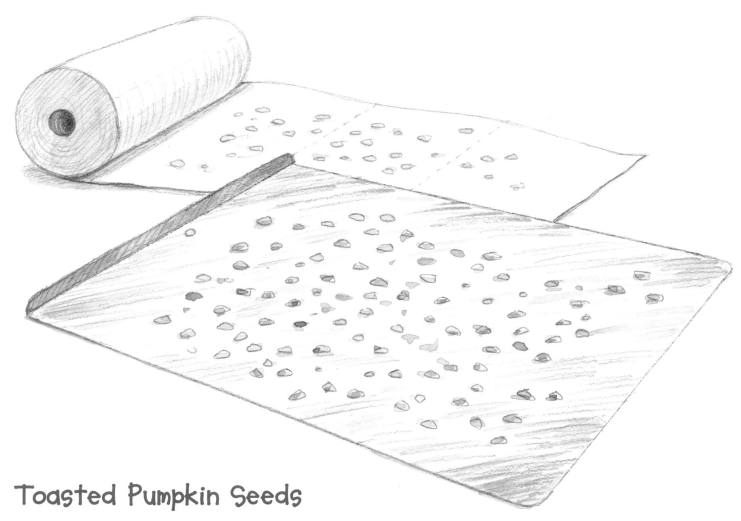

## Toasted Pumpkin Seeds

Preheat oven to 300 degrees.
Wash the pumpkin seeds and dry them on paper towels.
Spread the dry seeds on a cookie sheet.
Sprinkle with salt.
Sprinkle with curry powder, garlic powder, chili powder,
    or your favorite spice.
Roast for about 30 minutes, or until golden brown, stirring occasionally.

# What would you call a pumpkin if you lived in...

Italy—zucca (ZOOK-ka)
Japan—kabocha (kah-boh-cha)
Mexico—calabaza (kah-lah-BAH-sa)
Russia—tykva (TEEK-va)
China—nangua (NAHN-gwah)
Germany—Kürbis (KYEER-bis)
Turkey—balkabaği (BAHL-kah-bah)
France—citrouille (sit-ROO-yuh)
Iran—kadu tanbal (KA-doo TAN-bal)
The Netherlands—pompoen (pom-PEHN)
Sweden—pumpa (POOM-pa)
Brazil—abóbora (ah-BOH-boo-rah)

# Did you know?

### World's Heaviest Pumpkin

1,337.6 pounds, grown by Charles Houghton,
New Boston, New Hampshire, 2002

### World's Largest Pumpkin Pie

350 pounds, 5 feet in diameter, Circleville, Ohio, 1998

### Largest Number of Carved Pumpkins, All Lighted with Candles

28,952
Keene (New Hampshire)
Pumpkin Festival, 2003

### World Champion Carver

In 1999 Jerry Ayers of Baltimore, Ohio,
carved one ton of pumpkins with detailed designs
in 7 hours and 11 minutes! Whew!

### World's Fastest Carver

Steve Clarke of Havertown, Pennsylvania,
carved a single pumpkin in
1 minute, 14.8 seconds, in 2000.

# Find out more about pumpkins!

## Books

Cook, Deanna F. *Kids' Pumpkin Projects: Planting & Harvest Fun*. Charlotte, VT: Williamson Publishing Company, 1998.

Cuyler, Margery. *The All-Around Pumpkin Book*. New York: Holt, Rinehart and Winston, 1980.

Damerow, Gail. *The Perfect Pumpkin*. Pownal, VT: Storey Publishing, 1997.

Elffers, Joost and Saxton Freymann. *Play with Your Pumpkins*. Text by Johannes van Dam. New York: Stewart, Tabori & Chang Publishers, 1998.

Gibbons, Gail. *The Pumpkin Book*. New York: Holiday House, 1999.

Langevin, Don. *How-To-Grow World Class Giant Pumpkins II*. Norton, MA: Annedawn Publishing, 1998.

## Web sites

Remember, Web sites can change. Try running a search for "pumpkin" on your favorite search engine.

Pumpkin Nook
http://www.pumpkinnook.com/kidstuff.htm
Pumpkin jokes, songs, "create your own pumpkin," and links to other pumpkin sites

The Pumpkin Patch
http://www.pumpkin-patch.com
Lots of good pumpkin links

Virtual Jack-O'-Lantern
http://www.thepumpkinfarm.com/jack/jackboard.html
Pick your features and make a pumpkin

Pumpkins for Kids
http://home.inreach.com/kfarrell/pumpkin.html
Pumpkin facts, songs, crafts, and growing information

World Class Giant Pumpkin Home Page
http://www.backyardgardener.com/wcgp/index.html
Mostly for grownups, but with lots of information on giant pumpkins